A Prophet's Heart

Avoiding the Doorway to Deception

Jennifer LeClaire

Author of *The Heart of the Prophetic*

Unless otherwise noted, Scripture quotations are taken from the King James version of the Bible.

A Prophet's Heart: Avoiding the Doorway to Deception

Copyright © Jennifer LeClaire 2009

Published by Jennifer LeClaire Ministries

P.O. Box 3953

Hallandale Beach, Fla. 33008

www.jenniferleclaire.org

All rights reserved. No part of this publication may be reproduced, stored in a retrieval system, or transmitted in any form or by any means, electronic, mechanical, photocopying, scanning, or otherwise, except as permitted under Section 107 or 108 of the 1976 United States Copyright Act, without the prior written permission of the Publisher. Requests to the Publisher for permission should be addressed to the Permissions Department, Jennifer LeClaire Ministries, P.O. Box 3953, Hallandale Beach, Fla. 33000. E-mail jennifer@jenniferleclaire.org. Jennifer LeClaire's books are available at most Christian bookstores.

Dedication

This book is dedicated to every prophet who refuses to compromise God's will, who's willing to pay the price no matter how great, and who's willing to seek the truth no matter how hard. God bless you.

Table of Contents

Chapter 1: Do False Prophet Start Out False? 11

Chapter 2: Balaam's Big But 19

Chapter 3: Who's Eyes Will You Trust? 27

Chapter 4: The Reprobate Prophet 37

Chapter 5: The Narrow Way 45

Chapter 6: Signs and Wonders? 49

Chapter 7: Eye-Opening Insights 53

Chapter 8: Exposing the Spirits 57

Chapter 9: Facing Down the Tempter 59

Chapter 10: Avoiding Strange Fire 65

Chapter 11: A Prophetic Showdown 71

Afterword & Prayer 79

Preface

This genesis of this book was originally the 13th chapter of *The Heart of the Prophetic*. I wrote *The Heart of the Prophetic* to shine a bright light on some of the character flaws that cause prophets – and all believers, for that matter – to stray from the narrow path that leads to life and on to the broad path that leads to destruction. The book aimed to help us unlock a greater prophetic anointing so we can lead believers into greater maturity and turns the hearts of the children back to the Father.

The Heart of the Prophetic received rave reviews and commendations from many major, proven, time-tested apostolic and prophetic leaders in the Body of Christ, including Ernest Gentile, Dr. Bill Hamon and Graham Cooke. I was humbled to read what they wrote about the content of the book and I am still humbled when I come across those words.

When it was time to print *The Heart of the Prophetic*, I made a last minute decision to hold the 13th chapter. I wasn't sure my readers were ready to hear what the Holy Ghost was saying. Considering some of the unfortunate events in the apostolic and prophetic movement, however, I believe it's time to deliver this message. The Lord once said this to Jeremiah the prophet:

> I have heard what the prophets said, that prophesy lies in my name, saying, I have dreamed, I have dreamed. How long shall this be in the heart of the prophets that

> prophesy lies? yea, they are prophets of the deceit of their own heart; Which think to cause my people to forget my name by their dreams which they tell every man to his neighbour, as their fathers have forgotten my name for Baal.
>
> Jeremiah 23:25-27

Whether you are a prophet or a prophetic person, you need to examine your heart regularly. What's in our hearts affects the prophetic flow – and that could impact lives, even nations. Let us not speak a vision out of our own heart, but only out of the heart of the Lord.

When I look around at much of prophetic ministry at the time of this writing, I feel like Jeremiah when he recorded these words, "Mine heart within me is broken because of the prophets; all my bones shake; I am like a drunken man, and like a man whom wine hath overcome, because of the Lord, and because of the words of his holiness. For the land is full of adulterers; for because of swearing the land mourneth; the pleasant places of the wilderness are dried up, and their course is evil, and their force is not right. For both prophet and priest are profane; yea, in my house have I found their wickedness, saith the Lord" (Jeremiah 23:9-11).

And yet my heart is also hopeful. For I know that just as Elijah was not the only true prophet in a land of corruption, the Lord has a great army of prophets which have not bowed a knee unto Baal (1 Kings

19:18). Some of these prophets have been shunned by the Church. Others have yet to emerge from the wilderness. Still others are in the making process. In fact, some of them I count as friends and mentors.

I thank God that you are reading this book. I pray that you will open your eyes and ears and allow the Holy Ghost to show you anything that stands between you and your prophetic destiny. The psalmist said, "The statutes of the Lord are right, rejoicing the heart: the commandment of the Lord is pure, enlightening the eyes" (Psalm 19:8). And again, "Who can say, I have made my heart clean, I am pure from sin?" (Proverbs 20:9). And again, "Blessed are the pure in heart: for they shall see God" (Matthew 5:8).

Chapter 1

Do False Prophets Start Out False?

Examine and test and evaluate your own selves to see whether you are holding to your faith and showing the proper fruits of it. Test and prove yourselves [not Christ]. Do you not yourselves realize and know [thoroughly by an ever-increasing experience] that Jesus Christ is in you – unless you are [counterfeits] disapproved on trial and rejected?

2 Corinthians 13:5 (AMP)

Let me start with a bold statement. I don't believe false prophets start off as false prophets. I believe they start off on the right track, with zeal and fervor for the Lord, with a hunger for His voice, and with a determination to build the Kingdom of God. Unfortunately, some genuine, God-called prophets end up on the road of deception.

A false prophet is not merely someone who delivers an inaccurate word. A false prophet is someone who sets out to deceive, and is himself deceived.

Some who call themselves prophets were never called to be prophets to begin with. They took on the title, either because they coveted the calling, or because someone erroneously prophesied a prophetic mantle upon them earlier in life, or even because they truly felt that was what the Lord was calling them to – but they missed it. Many of them never understood true prophetic ministry and therefore never truly operated in the true prophetic anointing, which goes well beyond personal prophecy.

This is a sad testimony, and it's a cry for instruction in the prophetic. The Prophet Samuel had schools of prophets where he raised them up in the ways and will of God. Some prophetic training centers we see today merely teach out to activate spiritual gifts and sound spiritual while delivering a prophecy. That's missing the mark.

The Purpose of Prophetic Ministry

First, the New Testament prophet's primary function is not to stand under a spotlight in the midst of the minstrel's melodies and announce what says the Spirit of God. The New Testament prophet is not called to pronounce judgments and curses on cities, nations and people. In the New Testament, the primary purpose of the prophet is found in the Book of Ephesians:

> And he gave some, apostles; and some, prophets; and some, evangelists; and some, pastors and teachers; For the perfecting of the saints, for the work of the ministry, for the edifying of the body

of Christ: Till we all come in the unity of the faith, and of the knowledge of the Son of God, unto a perfect man, unto the measure of the stature of the fulness of Christ....

> Ephesians 4:11-13

In short, the New Testament prophet is not called function in all the same ways as Old Testament prophets. After all, we have a better covenant based on better promises. God didn't change but His covenant did – and so did His purpose for His prophets. Old Testament prophets primarily foretold the Messiah's coming and warned the Israelites about the ultimate consequences of following other gods.

Of course, that is not to say that New Testament prophets will not prophesy over a congregation or in a prayer line as the minstrels help to usher in the spirit of prophesy. It doesn't mean that New Testament prophets won't deliver true rebukes of the Spirit, either. What we have to keep in mind when we look at the heart of the prophetic in New Testament times is the covenant. Jesus Christ is the Prophet and He is our prototype. As a New Testament prophet, His primary function was to equip people for works of service in the Kingdom of God. Jesus taught His disciples. He prepared them for the ministry they would inherit after He ascended to the right hand of the Father.

Now that we have that out of the way, it is clear that the New Testament and Old Testament prophets do share some common functions. In those common functions, I believe, you will find the heart of the prophetic. I dive deeper into each of one of these areas in *The Heart of the Prophetic*, but I'll list them here for quick reference: standing in the gap, turning hearts, reforming, preparing a people for the Lord, and separating the profane from the holy.

When the Real Turns False

While minor character flaws may merely cause you to prophesy less accurately than you otherwise could – and that's a shame in and of itself – more serious character issues left unaddressed can lead the true into the realm of the false.

Balaam is perhaps a familiar example. But let us not get so familiar with his mistake that we overlook the warnings within it. God recorded these events so that we can learn from them, not merely so we can judge Balaam for his error.

First, it's noteworthy that there is no indication that Balaam was a false prophet when he is first mentioned in the Bible. In fact, the Jewish historian Josephus called him "the greatest of the prophets at that time." Now that's a recommendation!

Josephus goes on to tell the story of Balaam and Balak, the king of the Midianites who was hell bent on finding a way to overcome Israel. Balak sent ambassadors to Balaam to entreat the prophet to come to them so that he would pronounce curses to the destroy Israel. In Josephus' chronicle, Balaam treats the ambassadors kindly and inquired with God to determine His will. Let's look at the story from the Bible itself.

> Balak's messengers, who were elders of Moab and Midian, set out with money to pay Balaam to place a curse upon Israel. They went to Balaam and delivered Balak's message to him. "Stay here overnight," Balaam said. "In the morning I will tell you whatever the Lord directs me to say." So the officials from Moab stayed there with Balaam.
>
> That night God came to Balaam and asked him, "Who are these men visiting you?"
>
> Balaam said to God, "Balak son of Zippor, king of Moab, has sent me this message: Look, a vast horde of people has arrived from Egypt, and they cover the face of the earth. Come and curse these people for me. Then perhaps I will be able to stand up to them and drive them from the land.'"
>
> But God told Balaam, "Do not go with them. You are not to curse these people, for they have been blessed!" The next morning Balaam got up and told Balak's officials, "Go on home! The Lord will not let me go with you."
>
> Numbers 22:7-12 (NLT)

Balaam was obedient to the Lord's will. At this point, he was not willing to compromise. Balak's response was to send more distinguished men with more money. That's what the devil does. If he can't tempt you with something small, he'll attempt to tempt you with something greater.

The Contempt of Temptation

Satan tried to tempt Jesus to turn a stone into a piece of bread before he attempted to woo with a promise to rule the kingdoms of the world (Luke 4). He'll do the same with you. He'll start off with a small temptation; a tiny compromise. It may seem insignificant at some level – but God is watching to see what you will do. Will you stand by your God, or will you stoop down to the devil's level?

When you are tempted, exercise your faith. Is your faith strong enough to overcome temptation? In his letter to the Thessalonians, Paul was concerned about the faith of his spiritual sons and daughters. He longed to visit them, but Satan thwarted him more than once. So he sent faithful Timothy to see how they were faring amid the persecution and temptations of the enemy to once again serve idols instead of the one living God. Let's listen in:

> When I could bear [the suspense] no longer, I sent that I might learn [how you were standing the strain, and the endurance of] your faith, [for I was fearful] lest somehow the tempter had tempted

you and our toil [among you should prove to] be fruitless and to no purpose.

> 1 Thessalonians 3:5 (AMP)

What I want to point out to you is this: it takes faith to overcome temptations. When your flesh is rising up against you, put your faith to work to overcome. When your mind is under siege with vain imaginations, put your faith to work to overcome. When circumstances rise up to mock you, put your faith to work to overcome.

You have overcoming faith. How do you put it to work? One way is by speaking the Word out of your mouth and believing that it carries an anointing to break yokes and remove burdens.

When you speak the Word in faith, it produces more faith by the hearing of it. When you speak the Word in faith, you are resisting the devil and he must flee. When you speak the Word in faith, you are relying on God instead of yourself.

So next time temptation to doubt, temptation to flesh out, or some other kind of temptation comes at you, exercise your faith. Stop the devil dead in his tracks. Exercise your faith. Remember this:

> No temptation has seized you except what is common to man. And God is faithful; he will not let you be tempted beyond what you can bear. But when you are

tempted, he will also provide a way out so that you can stand up under it.

> 1 Corinthians 10:13

And remember, the same devil that tempted you will be right there to heap condemnation on you when he succeeds. If you need more help along these lines, check out my book "Doubtless: Faith that Overcomes the World." We'll also talk more about this in the last chapter of this book.

Chapter 2

Balaam's Big But

For the love of money is a root of all kinds of evil. Some people, eager for money, have wandered from the faith and pierced themselves with many griefs.

1 TIMOTHY 6:10 (AMP)

Now back to Balaam. Balaam's to the dignitaries who tempted him with riches was: "Even if Balak were to give me his palace filled with silver and gold, I would be powerless to do anything against the will of the Lord my God, but…" (Numbers 22:18)

It was the "but" that revealed Balaam's heart. God had already told Balaam not to go with the Midianites and not to curse Israel. That should have settled the matter. But Balaam opened the case with the Lord again. The fact that Balaam was willing to go to God about the matter a second time – and the fact that he was talking about silver, gold and palaces, speaks volumes. Balaam had greed in his heart. He wanted to collect on Balak's offer. The fact that he didn't collect makes no difference. His heart belied his allegiance to Jehovah.

Consider Paul the Apostle's warning to Timothy in this light:

> A devout life does bring wealth, but it's the rich simplicity of being yourself before God. Since we entered the world penniless and will leave it penniless, if we have bread on the table and shoes on our feet, that's enough.
>
> But if it's only money these leaders are after, they'll self-destruct in no time. Lust for money brings trouble and nothing but trouble. Going down that path, some lose their footing in the faith completely and live to regret it bitterly ever after.
>
> 1 Timothy 6:6-10 (MSG)

Balaam would live to regret his choice, but the Tempter worked him over. Balaam reopened the matter with God after the enemy sweetened the pot. God told him to go with the men, but only to do what He instructed. But the Bible says God was angry about it. I believe God wanted to see what Balaam would do. Balaam could have repented right then and there. He could have decided to stay with God's original plan and avoided the woes ahead. The situation reminds me of an experience Abraham had.

God tested Abraham to see what was in his heart when He told Abraham to sacrifice his son Isaac. Abraham, of course, passed the test with flying colors. He lost nothing. He didn't have to sacrifice his son. But he won God's trust at a new level. Balaam had this same opportunity; an opportunity to come up higher in the things of God. Already recognized as one of the greatest prophets in the land, this was Balaam's opportunity to increase his prophetic anointing.

God tested Balaam to see what was in his heart, but Balaam wasn't willing to sacrifice riches and honor for the will of the Lord. Balaam failed the test – and he failed it miserably. He may have been saying the right things out of his mouth – "I can only say what the Lord tells me" – but the abundant greed of his heart was speaking volumes on his behalf.

Balaam's Besmirched Legacy

Balaam didn't start out as a false prophet. He was one of the greatest prophets of his time, according to Josephus. That says a lot considering he lived in the days of Moses. But it just goes to show you that the anointing may take you where your character can't keep you. Don't ever let that happen. Get your character straight so you can use the anointing God has given you to bless and curse not.

Balaam was a great prophet, an authentic prophet. But he goes down in Bible history as a false prophet. Peter, Jude and even Jesus Himself spoke of Balaam.

> Which have forsaken the right way, and are gone astray, following the way of Balaam the son of Bosor, who loved the wages of unrighteousness; But was

rebuked for his iniquity: the dumb ass speaking with man's voice forbad the madness of the prophet. These are wells without water, clouds that are carried with a tempest; to whom the mist of darkness is reserved for ever.

> 2 Peter 2:5-17

But these speak evil of those things which they know not: but what they know naturally, as brute beasts, in those things they corrupt themselves. Woe unto them! for they have gone in the way of Cain, and ran greedily after the error of Balaam for reward, and perished in the gainsaying of Core. These are spots in your feasts of charity, when they feast with you, feeding themselves without fear: clouds they are without water, carried about of winds; trees whose fruit withereth, without fruit, twice dead, plucked up by the roots;

> Jude 1:10-12

I know thy works, and where thou dwellest, even where Satan's seat is: and thou holdest fast my name, and hast not denied my faith, even in those days wherein Antipas was my faithful martyr, who was slain among you, where Satan dwelleth.

> But I have a few things against thee, because thou hast there them that hold the doctrine of Balaam, who taught Balac to cast a stumblingblock before the children of Israel, to eat things sacrificed unto idols, and to commit fornication.
>
> Revelation 2:13-15

A Holy Ghost Warning

Of course, I believe the Holy Spirit warns us repeatedly when we are about to make a mistake. He loves us, and He doesn't want to see us suffer the consequences of our sin – and there are consequences even when we repent. At the least, sin temporarily distracts us from functioning in our calling. At the worst, sin takes us completely out of our destiny.

Yes, I do believe the Holy Spirit warns us through conviction, through the voices of mentors and counselors, and through the truth in the Word of God. It's when we refuse to submit to the leading of the Holy Spirit that we risk erring on the side of diviners, soothsayers and sorcerers. The Spirit of God will not always strive with man (Genesis 6:3). God is long-suffering, but He has given us a free will and we can choose to let Him help us avoid unrighteousness – or we can choose to enter into it.

Examine Your Heart

The Bible says we should examine ourselves and the concept of looking at one's own heart is mentioned more than once. David cried out to the Lord, "Examine me, O Lord, and prove me; try my reigns and my heart" (Psalm 26:2).

The Apostle Paul warned the Corinthians to examine themselves before they took communion, "for whosoever shall eat this bread, and drink this cup of the Lord, unworthily, shall be guilty of the body and the blood of the Lord" (1 Corinthians 11:27-28). Paul didn't stop there. He went on to say that "he that eateth and drinketh unworthily, eateth and drinketh damnation to himself, not discerning the Lord's body" (1 Corinthians 11:29).

I like the Message translation of 2 Corinthians 12:4-6:

> Test yourselves to make sure you are solid in the faith. Don't drift along taking everything for granted. Give yourselves regular checkups. You need firsthand evidence, not mere hearsay, that Jesus Christ is in you. Test it out. If you fail the test, do something about it. I hope the test won't show that we have failed. But if it comes to that, we'd rather the test showed our failure than yours. We're rooting for the truth to win out in you. We couldn't possibly do otherwise.

Do you hear the Holy Spirit? Examine yourself right now. Make sure your faith is solid. Greed is not the only character pitfall. I used greed in this chapter to illustrate a true prophet's fall into false prophethood. You can read about the other major assignments against prophets and prophetic people in my book *The Heart of the Prophetic*.

Examine yourself. If you fail the test, do something about it. Repent. Change your way of thinking. Change your life. The Father, Son and Holy Spirit are rooting for you – and so am I.

Chapter 3

Who's Eyes Will You Trust?

The light of the body is the eye: if therefore thine eye be single, thy whole body shall be full of light. But if thine eye be evil, thy whole body shall be full of darkness. If therefore the light that is in thee be darkness, how great is that darkness!

MATTHEW 6:22-23

Did you examine yourself? If you didn't take the time to pray and ask the Holy Spirit to show you any places within your heart that need to be realigned to His will, please don't put it off any longer. This book isn't going anywhere. It's important for you to examine your heart. Here's why: I believe false prophets are first deceived themselves before they set out to deceive others. It's a web of deception that's tangled indeed.

Now, it's possible to examine yourself and still not see the deception. That's the nature of deception and it works with pride to keep you from seeing the truth, especially if you aren't really willing to see it. When we are deceived, it's akin to wearing spiritual blinders. Do you know why they put blinders on a horse? So the horse will stay focused on what's just ahead. The blinders limit or obstruct the horse's vision. When we are deceived, spiritual blinders obstruct our discernment – and we don't see the devil working.

Chances are, if you are deceived, you probably don't know it. I speak from experience. God will use some interesting methods to get through to His prophets. One time, He even sent a whale to pick up a prophet to get his attention. I'm grateful God didn't have to go that far with me. Instead, he sent a blind man. I was in the elevator thinking to myself how unfair my situation was, how mistreated I had been. I was having a five-star pity party with me, myself and I. But I was also searching for answers. I was asking God to show me if I was somehow wrong. (Of course, I was sure I was right and was only half-heartedly asking to see the truth. But at least I asked! Ultimately, I did want truth.)

Anyway, I was in the elevator pouting when lo and behold the door opened and a blind man walked in. I mean storybook blind man. He had the dark glasses, the red and white cane with the vibrating tip and everything. He stumbled around a bit to get into the elevator and he never said a word. I had never seen him before and I never saw him again. Though there were no words exchanged, I could hear God speaking clearly. "Uh-oh, I'm completely blind about my situation," I thought. Suffice it to say I repented and got back on track in a hurry and today I can almost laugh about God sending a blind man to teach me a lesson.

Here's my point: If you set your will to examine yourself – and you are ready to repent for what the Lord reveals – then it opens up your lines of communication with the Spirit of God without the static sin creates.

The Man in the Mirror

Self-deception has got to be the worst brand of deception. So if you are reading this book, don't blow over the biblical mandate to examine yourself. The Word of God is a mirror. Listen to how James the apostle spells it out:

> Do not merely listen to the word, and so deceive yourselves. Do what it says. Anyone who listens to the word but does not do what it says is like a man who looks at his face in a mirror and, after looking at himself, goes away and immediately forgets what he looks like. But the man who looks intently into the perfect law that gives freedom, and continues to do this, not forgetting what he has heard, but doing it—he will be blessed in what he does.
>
> James 1:22-25

We all need to examine ourselves – and frequently. We need to stay in a humble state of reliance on God and repentance for sin. When we look in the mirror that is the Word of God, we will see that we are called to be the righteousness of God in Christ Jesus. But are we walking in that righteousness or are we compromising with the world?

When we look in the mirror of the Word of God, we will see that we are called to walk in love with our brothers and sisters. But are we obeying the command or do we manifest selfishness at every turn?

When we look in the mirror of the Word of God, we see that we are not supposed to let any corrupt communication come out of our mouth, but only that which is helpful for building others up according to their needs, that it might benefit those who listen (Ephesians 4:29). But are we speaking words we'll want to give account for on the Judgment Day? Are we really?

You get the picture. Don't wait for the Holy Spirit to nudge you apart from the Word. Yes, He certainly can and probably has tried to get your attention, but if you are wrapped in a Web of deception your spiritual senses may be too dull to hear His voice.

That's another reason why the written Word of God is so important. The Word and the Spirit work together. The Spirit will reveal the Word. Don't abandon one for the other. The Word is a lamp unto your feet and if you walk in it you'll steer clear of Satan's dark path.

One more thing: Don't be too quick to say your heart is clean without examining yourself. If we say we have no sin, we deceive ourselves, and the truth is not in us (1 John 1:8). But thank God if we confess our sins, He is faithful and just to forgive us our sins, and to cleanse us from all unrighteousness (1 John 1:9).

Don't deceive yourself. Look at yourself through God's eyes. Let the Word of God serve as a mirror. We don't know the end from the beginning as God does. What we do know is all the ways of a man seem pure in his own eyes, but the Lord weighs the thoughts and intents of the heart (Proverbs 16:2). We also know that the way of a fool is right in his own eyes: but he that hearkeneth unto counsel is wise (Proverbs 12:15). Hearken unto the counsel of the Holy Ghost. Hearken unto the counsel of the Word. And hearken unto the counsel of mature leaders who aren't to timid to speak the truth in love.

Don't Be Squinty-Eyed

See, we can't trust our own eyes if our eyes aren't single. Jesus said the light of the body is the eye, therefore when your eyes are good your whole body is filled with light (Matthew 6:22-23). But when they are bad, your body also is full of darkness. I like the way The Message drives the point across:

> If you live wide-eyed in wonder and belief, your body fills up with light. If you live squinty-eyed in greed and distrust, your body is a dank cellar. Keep

> your eyes open, your lamp burning, so you don't get musty and murky. Keep your life as well-lighted as your best-lighted room.

Again, God's word is a lamp unto our feet and a light unto our paths (Psalm 119). If we acknowledge Him in all our ways, He will direct our steps. His eyes see everything. In fact, the Bible says His eyes are roaming to and fro throughout the whole earth to show Himself strong on behalf of them whose heart is perfect toward Him (2 Chronicles 16:9). Let that be you.

When the Son of Man returns will He find faith on the earth? (Luke 18:8) Or will He find politically correct, merchandising controllers – fruit that is rotten to the core rather than faith that endures to the end? I reckon He will find some of both because Jesus said the Kingdom of heaven is like a net that catches all kinds of fish.

> When it was full, the fishermen pulled it up on the shore. Then they sat down and collected the good fish in baskets, but threw the bad away. This is how it will be at the end of the age. The angels will come and separate the wicked from the righteous and throw them into the fiery furnace, where there will be weeping and gnashing of teeth
>
> Matthew 13:47-50 (NIV)

Resisting the Pressure of Prophetic Ministry

There is a certain pressure that comes with prophetic ministry. There is the pressure of facing rejection after rejection after rejection. We see God's prophets face rejection in the Bible, from Moses to Jesus and many in between. We can withstand this pressure by following Jesus' example.

We know that if we are prophesying what Jesus is really saying and we are afterward rejected, it is really Jesus they are rejecting, not us. Our response should be to bless those who curse us and pray for those who despitefully use us. Jesus said "If the world hates you, keep in mind that they hated me first" (John 15:18). So keep that in mind when you face the pain of rejection.

The pressure of persecution also comes with prophetic ministry. The Apostle James said, "[As] an example of suffering and ill-treatment together with patience, brethren, take the prophets who spoke in the name of the Lord [as His messengers]" (James 5:10).

I always note how James didn't say to take the apostles, evangelists, pastors and teachers as an example of suffering. He put a spotlight on prophetic ministry. That's not to imply that every believer doesn't face persecution. But there's something about the voice of God that brings out the best – and the worst – in people.

We can resist the pressure of persecution by once again following Jesus' example. He said a couple of things about persecution. First, Jesus said, "Blessed are they which are persecuted for righteousness' sake: for theirs is the kingdom of heaven" (Matthew 5:9). It helps to remember that you are blessed and an exceedingly great reward is awaiting you. Jesus also said this:

> Blessed are ye, when men shall revile you, and persecute you, and shall say all manner of evil against you falsely, for my sake. Rejoice, and be exceeding glad: for great is your reward in heaven: for so persecuted they the prophets which were before you.
>
> Matthew 5:11-12

My friends, I'm quite sure you'll never have it as bad as Jeremiah or Isaiah. The type of persecution most of us face doesn't compare to what the prophets of old experienced. Still, I understand all too well the sting of having someone who is supposed to be a brother or sister in Christ – as well as spiritually dead people from the world – revile you, accuse you, put words in your mouth and the like. That's why I also take comfort in what the Apostle Peter said. I hope this will relieve some of the pressure you face as well:

> Beloved, think it not strange concerning the fiery trial which is to try you, as though some strange thing happened unto you: But rejoice, inasmuch as ye are partakers of Christ's sufferings; that, when his glory shall be revealed, ye may be glad also with exceeding joy. If ye be reproached for the name of Christ, happy are ye; for the spirit

> of glory and of God resteth upon you: on their part he is evil spoken of, but on your part he is glorified.
>
> 1 Peter 4:12-14

There is also the pressure of resisting the temptation toward pride – or even false humility. Knowledge puffs up, but love builds up (1 Corinthians 8:1). The knowledge one receives as part of the prophetic gift can lead to pride if we don't actively resist it. Once again, we look to Christ as our example.

> Let this mind be in you, which was also in Christ Jesus: Who, being in the form of God, thought it not robbery to be equal with God: But made himself of no reputation, and took upon him the form of a servant, and was made in the likeness of men: And being found in fashion as a man, he humbled himself, and became obedient unto death, even the death of the cross.
>
> Philippians 2:5-8

Don't allow pride to lead you into the wrong boat. Stay on the Lord's side. You don't want to wake up on the other side of eternity one day and try to convince the Lord that you should gain entrance into the Kingdom of heaven because you prophesied in His name, cast out devils in His name, and in His name did many mighty miracles, only to hear Him say He never knew you and command you to leave His presence (Matthew 7:22-24).

Chapter 4

The Reprobate Prophet

Now as Jannes and Jambres withstood Moses, so do these also resist the truth: men of corrupt minds, reprobate concerning the faith. But they shall proceed no further: for their folly shall be manifest unto all men, as their's also was.

2 TIMOTHY 3:7-9

God may have no choice but to give some prophets over to a reprobate mind (Romans 1:28). A reprobate mind is one that is morally corrupt and rejected as worthless or not standing a test. A reprobate mind is one that is condemned strongly as unacceptable or evil. That sounds harsh, but the Bible offers a clear warning to those who do not see fit to acknowledge God. Let's listen in to this dire warning:

> And even as they did not like to retain God in their knowledge, God gave them over to a reprobate mind, to do those things which are not convenient; Being filled with all unrighteousness, fornication, wickedness, covetousness, maliciousness;

> full of envy, murder, debate, deceit, malignity; whisperers,
>
> Backbiters, haters of God, despiteful, proud, boasters, inventors of evil things, disobedient to parents, Without understanding, covenantbreakers, without natural affection, implacable, unmerciful: Who knowing the judgment of God, that they which commit such things are worthy of death, not only do the same, but have pleasure in them that do them.
>
> Romans 1:28-32

Once God turns someone over to a reprobate mind, the fruit of that one's life is pure wickedness. This was not the only instance when the Apostle Paul talked about reprobates. He also warned Timothy to stay away from this kind who are reprobate concerning the faith. Compare Paul's description of a reprobate in Romans to what he tells Timothy:

> This know also, that in the last days perilous times shall come. For men shall be lovers of their own selves, covetous, boasters, proud, blasphemers, disobedient to parents, unthankful, unholy, Without natural affection, trucebreakers, false accusers, incontinent, fierce, despisers of those that are good, Traitors, heady, highminded, lovers of pleasures more than lovers of God;

> Having a form of godliness, but denying the power thereof: from such turn away. For of this sort are they which creep into houses, and lead captive silly women laden with sins, led away with divers lusts, Ever learning, and never able to come to the knowledge of the truth.
>
> Now as Jannes and Jambres withstood Moses, so do these also resist the truth: men of corrupt minds, reprobate concerning the faith. But they shall proceed no further: for their folly shall be manifest unto all men, as theirs also was.
>
> 2 Timothy 3:1-9

I hope this is stirring you. I hope this is making you think. I hope this is encouraging you to examine your heart. Even the thought of being classified with the reprobates is enough to strike the fear of the Lord in me and send me to the mirror of the Word of God. In case you need another witness, consider what Paul told his other spiritual son, Titus.

> Unto the pure all things are pure: but unto them that are defiled and unbelieving is nothing pure; but even their mind and conscience is defiled. They profess that they know God; but in works they deny

him, being abominable, and disobedient, and unto every good work reprobate.

Titus 1:15-16

Simon the Gnostic

In his discussion of reprobates, Paul was railing against enemies of the truth. He was battling the onslaught of Gnosticism in the early Church – and we're still fighting that battle today. According to the Encyclopedia Britannica, consensus on a definition of Gnosticism has proved difficult. But here is what the encyclopedia says about it:

> Many of the so-called Gnostic groups are characterized by a mythology that distinguishes between an inferior creator of the world (a demiurge) and a more transcendent god or order of being. Another frequently encountered theme is that there is a special class or race of humans that is descended from the transcendent realm and is destined to achieve salvation and to return to its spiritual origins.

Simon the Sorcerer was a Gnostic. You'll remember him as the one who tried to buy the power of God. Listen in to this account, and as you do, consider how we've seen Christians trying to buy and sell the power of God in today's Church:

Now for some time a man named Simon had practiced sorcery in the city and amazed all the people of Samaria. He boasted that he was someone great, and all the people, both high and low, gave him their attention and exclaimed, "This man is the divine power known as the Great Power."

They followed him because he had amazed them for a long time with his magic. But when they believed Philip as he preached the good news of the kingdom of God and the name of Jesus Christ, they were baptized, both men and women. Simon himself believed and was baptized. And he followed Philip everywhere, astonished by the great signs and miracles he saw.

When the apostles in Jerusalem heard that Samaria had accepted the word of God, they sent Peter and John to them. When they arrived, they prayed for them that they might receive the Holy Spirit, because the Holy Spirit had not yet come upon any of them; they had simply been baptized into the name of the Lord Jesus.

Then Peter and John placed their hands on them, and they received the Holy Spirit.

> When Simon saw that the Spirit was given at the laying on of the apostles' hands, he offered them money and said, "Give me also this ability so that everyone on whom I lay my hands may receive the Holy Spirit."
>
> Peter answered: "May your money perish with you, because you thought you could buy the gift of God with money! You have no part or share in this ministry, because your heart is not right before God. Repent of this wickedness and pray to the Lord. Perhaps he will forgive you for having such a thought in your heart. For I see that you are full of bitterness and captive to sin."

You have to stand in the office of the prophet. While you stand, temptations will come. The goal of the enemy's temptation is to get you to compromise God's Word in your life. God is watching to see if you will choose the truth. Reprobates not only fail to choose the truth, reprobates resist the truth (2 Timothy 3:8). They profess to know God but their abominable, disobedient works deny them (Titus 1:16).

The Apostle Paul warned the church at Corinth to steer clear of this fate by examining themselves: "Examine yourselves, whether ye be in the faith; prove your own selves. Know ye not your own selves, how that Jesus Christ is in you, except ye be reprobates? (2 Corinthians 13:5).

I realize we just looked at this Scripture in the first chapter of the book, but it's such an important concept that we need to review it. I'd rather bring it to you 100 different ways than risk the chance that you miss this. Let's look at how the Amplified version spells it out:

> Examine and test and evaluate your own selves to see whether you are holding to your faith and showing the proper fruits of it. Test and prove yourselves [not Christ]. Do you not yourselves realize and know [thoroughly by an ever-increasing experience] that Jesus Christ is in you – unless you are [counterfeits] disapproved on trial and rejected?

Now, it should be noted that false prophets can offer up true prophetic utterances, which can keep the deceived in utter deception. If you are loath to address sin, if you are attracted to the concepts of accumulating wealth, power and prestige, if you are willing to compromise in any way, then you are in danger of becoming an evil imposter.

The Apostle Paul also said, "Everyone who wants to live a godly life in Christ Jesus will be persecuted, while evil men and impostors will go from bad to worse, deceiving and being deceived" (1 Timothy 2:12-13). Sounds like a false prophet to me.

Chapter 5

The Narrow Way

Enter ye in at the strait gate: for wide is the gate, and broad is the way, that leadeth to destruction, and many there be which go in thereat.

MATTHEW 7:13

The narrow way is full of persecution and apostles and prophets get their fair share of it. As I mentioned earlier, James said to consider the prophets who spoke in the name of the Lord as an example of patience in the face of suffering (James 5:10).

Notice he didn't say, take the pastors as an example or take the teachers as an example. He said take the prophets as an example. I'm not saying others don't suffer. We all suffer to do God's will, of course. But James singled out the prophets.

The gate that leads to destruction is wide and it has on its curbs praise of men and riches. The narrow is the way that leads to life if characterized by persecution and suffering. Which path will you choose?

Here's the bottom line: You will either suffer now or suffer later. It will be much worse later if you don't choose the narrow gate now. I like the way the Amplified Bible translates Jesus' words of truth:

> Enter through the narrow gate; for wide is the gate and spacious and broad is the way that leads away to destruction, and many are those who are entering through it. But the gate is narrow (contracted by pressure) and the way is straitened and compressed that leads away to life, and few are those who find it.
>
> Matthew 7:13-14

Notice the Amplified translation says the gate is narrow because it is "contracted by pressure." We discussed the pressure of prophetic ministry in the last chapter as it relates to critics and skeptics. But there is another kind of pressure that comes in the form of narrowing grace as we mature. In other words, what we got away with 15 years ago won't fly with the Lord today. He expects more of us, and sometimes we feel that pressure.

The definition of "pressure" is the constraint of circumstance. I take this to mean that God has a narrow path for His prophets to walk, perhaps narrower than the ordinary believer who does not carry the responsibility of restoring the hearts of the sons back to the fathers and the hearts of the feathers back to the sons; who does not have the task of equipping the saints to know the voice, will and mind of God;

who doesn't have the call to represent God's voice on the earth.

The way has to be narrow – and that leaves less room for error. If we stay on His narrow path, we will flow more accurately because we'll be walking with Him rather than behind or ahead of him, or even on a different path altogether.

What I find interesting about Matthew 7:13-14 is the verse that comes right after it. Jesus warns the disciples that the path to life is narrow and the path to destruction is broad and in the next breath he tells them to "Beware of false prophets, which come to you in sheep's clothing, but inwardly they are ravening wolves."

I don't think it is any coincidence that Jesus mentioned that few find the narrow gate and in the next breath He mentioned false prophets who dress up as God-fearing believers. We know false prophets by their fruits. As long as we're on this earth, it's never too late to bring forth fruit meet for repentance (Matthew 3:8).

Chapter 6

Signs and Wonders?

For false Christs and false prophets shall rise, and shall shew signs and wonders, to seduce, if it were possible, even the elect.

MATTHEW 7:13-14

Are you demonstrating great signs and wonders in the name of the Lord? That's not proof that your heart is clean. Jesus warned us in Matthew 24:24 that false Christs and false prophets would arise and show great signs and wonders insomuch that, if it were possible, they shall deceive the very elect. John warned us to "believe not every spirit, but try the spirits whether they are of God: because many false prophets are gone out into the world" (1 John 4:1).

Don't look at your miracle ministry to ease your conscious. That's not exactly what Jesus meant when He said you will know them by their fruit. Signs and wonders without salvations are only a partial success. When the lights go down and the music fades, do you walk in the fruit of the spirit or the fruit of the flesh? In other words, what goes on behind closed doors when no one is watching?

Even so every good tree bringeth forth good fruit; but a corrupt tree bringeth forth evil fruit. A good tree cannot bring forth evil fruit, neither can a corrupt tree bring forth good fruit. Every tree that bringeth not forth good fruit is hewn down, and cast into the fire.

Wherefore by their fruits ye shall know them. Not every one that saith unto me, Lord, Lord, shall enter into the kingdom of heaven; but he that doeth the will of my Father which is in heaven.

Many will say to me in that day, Lord, Lord, have we not prophesied in thy name? and in thy name have cast out devils? and in thy name done many wonderful works? And then will I profess unto them, I never knew you: depart from me, ye that work iniquity.

Matthew 7:17-23

I don't want to be deceived. I don't want to fall into the trap Peter fell into where one moment He was speaking under divine revelation and the next moment he was speaking under the inspiration of the devil. I know you don't, either. You wouldn't have made it this far to the book if you did. You were have gotten too angry after Chapter 1 to read any further.

Yet there comes a temptation so great that all but those who are completely submitted to the will of God and willing to sacrifice all at His command will fall to it. One of those temptations, as it has manifested in the last 100 years, is to think one is the actual Prophet Elijah.

There is a spirit that lays in wait at a certain level of the prophetic ministry. Don't think for a moment that it's not possible for you to be deceived. Jesus said, "Take heed that ye be not deceived" (Luke 21:8). The Pharisees knew the Word of God inside and out, but they were as deceived as you can get. The Apostle Paul warned, "Be not deceived" on several occasions (1 Corinthians 6:9, 1 Corinthians 15:33, Galatians 6:7). And he was talking to believers.

Don't be deceived by signs and wonders, whether they come at your hand or the hand of another. Consider the warning from the Apostle Paul found in 2 Thessalonians 2:9-12:

> Even him, whose coming is after the working of Satan with all power and signs and lying wonders, And with all deceivableness of unrighteousness in them that perish; because they received not the love of the truth, that they might be saved. And for this cause God shall send them strong delusion, that they should believe a lie: That they all might be damned who believed not the truth, but had pleasure in unrighteousness.

Chapter 7
Eye-Opening Insights

For all that is in the world, the lust of the flesh, and the lust of the eyes, and the pride of life, is not of the Father, but is of the world.

MATTHEW 7:17-23

There are many variations of the trio of sinful themes – the lust of the eyes, the lust of the flesh and the pride of life. In *The Heart of the Prophetic*, I focused on some of the more common character issues and ungodly roots that I've seen work their way into the prophetic ministry today. But these foundational traps can manifest in more ways than we may want to admit and this is by no means was my book an exhaustive study.

If you haven't read *The Heart of the Prophetic*, pick up a copy if you can handle the truth. It sets the stage for this book.

We can discern some additional early warning signs from the operations of false prophets mentioned in the Bible. False prophets bring damnable heresies (2 Peter 2:1).

Heresies are dissentions and deviations from the truth that lead people astray. Even today we see a split among prophetic camps with some dangerous implications. We've got to base our revelations on the Word of God – the whole counsel of the Word of God. The Holy Spirit doesn't contradict Himself. He does not speak with a forked tongue.

False prophets are reckless and irresponsible. They don't seem to care who they hurt. Before we open our mouths, we should be confident in the unction of the Lord. The Message Bible really puts this into context for today's Church:

> Oh yes, I've had it with the prophets who preach the lies they dream up, spreading them all over the country, ruining the lives of my people with their cheap and reckless lies. I never sent these prophets, never authorized a single one of them. They do nothing for this people – nothing!
>
> Jeremiah 23:32

I believe God even more fed up today with prophets who are touring the country with false visions, dreams, judgments and curses that are diverting the saints' attention from what the Spirit is really saying in this hour. I submit to you that if God's wrath was falling upon us, there would be no debate about it. We'd all be thoroughly convinced. Much of what we are seeing in the world today is consequences of sin, not judgment.

We are living in perilous times. People need to be equipped to hear from God, they need to be inspired to seek first the Kingdom of God and His righteousness. They don't need to be judged, damned, cursed or otherwise harassed by Jezebel- and Balaam-inspired prophets.

Chapter 8
Exposing the Spirits

Beloved, believe not every spirit, but try the spirits whether they are of God: because many false prophets are gone out into the world.

1 JOHN 4:1

False prophets are also adulterous, meaning they are unfaithful and willing to break covenants and agreements (Jeremiah 23:14). God demands complete faithfulness from His prophets, no matter what the cost. If you are friend of this world, you are an enemy of God.

False prophets are murderous, maligning the reputation of others to make themselves look good. It's one thing to call a sin a sin. It's another thing to assassinate someone's character for your own gain. This can be a thin line indeed. We must be led by the Spirit – not a spirit – but the Spirit.

We know that the Apostle Paul warned Timothy of false teachers. He also let him know that Demas deserted him because "he loved this present world" (2 Timothy 4:10). He also singled out Alexander the metalworker who did him harm and warned Timothy to "be on your guard against him because he strongly opposed our message" (2 Timothy 4:14-15). Even John, the Apostle of Love, warned of Diotrephes, who "loves to be first" and was gossiping maliciously about John and his company (3 John 1:9-10).

Prophets should warn the church of those who are hell bent on destroying God's work and perverting His voice. But it's the spirit behind the announcement. I believe that most often we can call out the deceived without naming names. It's enough to describe the actions and teach the truth. Do you know how they teach bankers to discern a counterfeit $100 bill? It's not by having them study counterfeit bills, as you would think. Rather, it's by having them study bona fide bills.

I believe we can discern the false even quicker by studying true prophets and their character, and I also believe we need to teach about what false prophets look like and call out their falsehoods. In his epistle to the Ephesians, Paul said the fruit of the Spirit is in all goodness and righteousness and truth, proving what is acceptable to the Lord. The Holy Ghost speaking through Paul warns us to "have no fellowship with the unfruitful works of darkness, but rather expose them" (Ephesians 5:11-12).

I like to put it this way: let's expose the spirits and let's expose the character flaws that open up the door to these spirits. That was the aim of *The Heart of the Prophetic* – and this book picks up where we left off with a clear warning to examine yourself. I hope you are hearing the Spirit of God in this.

Chapter 9

Facing Down the Tempter

When I could no longer foreberar, I sent to know your faith, lest by some means the tempter have tempted you, and our labor be in vain.

1 THESSALONIANS 3:5

As you stand in the office of a prophet you will face temptations at seasons in your life. Know that those temptations don't come from the Lord. They come from Satan.

Satan has many names – the Evil One, the Father of Lies, the Accuser of the Brethren. These are all aspects of his wicked character. But one of his names – the Tempter – describes the allure of sin in our lives.

Consider the great men and women of God who fell to the Tempter. Adam, Eve, David, Samson, Judas. The truth is we've all fallen short of the glory of God at the Tempter's beckoning. And it's time we face down this demon coaxer once and for all and tell him to get behind us!

The Tempter uses what's in us, of course, but let's get beyond the generic discussion about the flesh and the carnal mind. By the same token, let's not go the extreme of sexual sin or white collar Enron-style embezzlement. Chances are, the Tempter comes at you with subtler temptations that tap into soulish insecurities or impatience, especially when you are in a wilderness place.

The Strategies of Satan

The temptation could be a desire to prove your calling to the world at the wrong time. It could be a temptation to misuse the Word – or take it out of context – for personal gain or to prove a point. It could be a temptation to pursue the wrong kind of power or idolize the wrong god.

Indeed, these are the very strategies the Tempter used against Jesus when He was in the wilderness. You've probably heard it said that Satan doesn't have any new tricks. Well, I'm here to tell you he doesn't have any new temptations, either. It all boils down to the lust of the eyes, the lust of the flesh and the pride of life, doesn't it? (1 John 2:16).

Said in different words, wanting our own way, wanting everything for ourselves, and wanting to appear important opens the door to the Tempter. I believe if we can expose the Tempter we can defeat him. When we think we are beyond temptation – in any area – that the devil sneaks in and defeats God's will in our lives.

The Flesh Temptation

Jesus was full of the Holy Spirit. (How about you? Without the Holy Spirit's help, we'll never thwart the Tempter.) The Holy Spirit drove Jesus into the desert, where He was tempted by the Devil for 40 days. After Jesus fasted for about six weeks, the Tempter figured it was time for a flesh test. The Tempter said to Jesus: "If you are the Son of God, turn this stone into bread" (Luke 4:3).

This is interesting because the temptation came with a provocation. In other words, it was almost as if the devil was saying, "Prove your identity by using your power – I dare you!" The devil knew right well who Jesus was, and he knows who we are: sons and daughters of God with the authority to bind his wicked operations.

Has the Tempter ever challenged your identity or your ministry? Have you ever felt the need to prove who you are in Christ, or the authenticity of your God-given gift? One too many prophets have been tempted to prophesy in the midst of large, expectant crowds when there was no unction. Jesus wasn't into giving signs. He wasn't into proving Himself. We shouldn't be either.

Provocation aside, the first temptation sought to entice Jesus to use His powers for personal provision. Specifically, to create bread to satisfy His hungry belly. How many ministers of the Gospel have been tempted to use their charismatic gifts to meet their personal needs rather than to meet the needs of others and trust God for their own? Selah.

Jesus taught us how to respond to such temptations. Jesus answered by quoting Deuteronomy: "It is written, man does not live by bread alone but by every word that proceeds out of the mouth of God" (Luke 4:4). In other words, trust God's Word. He is the One who supplies all of our needs according to His riches in glory by Christ Jesus (Philippians 4:19).

The Wealth and Power Temptation

Next, the Devil led Jesus up to a high place and showed Him all the kingdoms of the world. The Tempter then promised to give Jesus all their authority and splendor if He would worship him (Luke 4:5). Bowing down to the Tempter would have meant Jesus could skirt the cross and go straight to the glory – worldly glory, that is.

I found it interesting that Jesus freely followed the Devil to a high place. He didn't have to go, but He went and submitted Himself to the temptation. (Yes, it was a temptation or the Bible wouldn't have called it a temptation.) I believe Jesus wanted us to have a heads up about one of the Devil's tricks: offers of worldly fame, glamour and riches in exchange for our worship. Remember, Satan is the god of this world (2 Corinthians 4:4) and many are worshipping him whether they know it or not.

Along with the cares and anxieties of the world, it's the distractions of the age, and the pleasure and delight and false glamour, and the deceitfulness of riches, and the craving and passionate desire for other things that creep in and choke the Word (Mark 4:19 AMP). If we fall to this temptation, our lives and ministries will be fruitless.

Sure, we may look juicy on the outside, but the inside will be dry and flavorless. When the Tempter comes with this tactic – and he will – we must respond like Jesus did. "Jesus refused, again backing his refusal with Deuteronomy: 'Worship the Lord your God and only the Lord your God. Serve him with absolute single-heartedness'" (Luke 4:8 MSG).

The Temptation to Twist the Word

When the Tempter failed on his first two cracks, he took the warfare to a whole new level. He sought to kill Jesus by tempting Him to use the Word of God inappropriately. The Devil finally caught on to Jesus' strategy of using the written Word to counter his temptations. So he adjusted his strategy mid-stream and used the Word itself against Jesus.

The Tempter took Jesus to Jerusalem and had Him stand on the highest point of the temple, saying, "If you are God's Son, jump. It's written, isn't it, that 'he has placed you in the care of angels to protect you; they will catch you; you won't so much as stub your toe on a stone'?" (Luke 4:9-11 MSG)

Can you rightly divide the Word of Truth? Remember, the Tempter knows the Word of God inside and out.

After all, he's had a lot longer to study it than we have. The Devil may misuse God's Word, written or prophetic, to deceive us. But let's flip that around for a moment. The Tempter will also tempt us to misuse the Word for our own benefit or to prove a point. That's called the spirit of error, and it comes with the temptation not to judge our "revelations." By the mouth of two or three witnesses shall every word be established (2 Corinthians 13:1).

Jesus knew just the right response to shut the devil up for good. He put the Tempter's seducing words into context, and said, "It is written, You shall not tempt the Lord thy God" (Luke 4:12). That shut him up alright, at least for a while. The Bible says the Tempter backed off. Sounds simple doesn't it?

Let's not think more highly of ourselves than we ought. Yes, we are more than conquerors in Christ Jesus, but even Superman had to deal with kryptonite. Our kryptonite is called the carnal nature. So when the Tempter comes, rise up in the Spirit, tell the devil who you really are and what the Word says. Remember, it is written in James 4:7, "Submit yourself to God, resist the devil and he will flee."

Chapter 10

Avoiding Strange Fire

And Nadab and Abihu, the sons of Aaron, took either of them his censer, and put fire therein, and put incense thereon, and offered strange fire before the Lord, which he commanded them not.

LEVITICUS 10:1

Kabbalah. Angel worship. Strange fire. These foreign practices have found their way into the Body of Christ and I'm sad to say the prophetic ministry is too often the door opener. It seems instead of prophets getting into the world, the world is getting into the prophets. The danger is false prophecies, false worship and even false revival.

I'm hardly surprised anymore when I go to the shopping mall and see a kiosk selling Kabbalah merchandise. I'm no longer shocked to learn of New Age cults or Satanic sects forming around angel worship. And the merchandising tactics on some Christian television broadcasts no longer astonishes me, though each of these practices stir my spirit to blow the trumpet all the louder.

Do we need greater discernment in the Body of Christ? If prophets were working to equip believers with prophetic grace, I submit to you Christians would indeed walk in greater discernment. Instead, we see some thieving Kingdom finances to fund extravagant lifestyles while millions of children around the world go hungry day in and day out, and millions of adults are on their way to hell.

We need to take a closer look at how we're prophesying, who we're worshipping and how we're praying – and if we're missing it we need to repent and get back to doing things God's way.

How about Kabbalah? The word literally means "receiving" and is deceiving because Kabbalahists are not hearing from the Spirit of God. In essence, the way some prophets exploit Kabbalah amounts to nothing more than demonic mysticism.

Those who prophesy with the guide of Kabbalah believe mastering this "receiving" will bring them spiritually closer to God. They use Kabbalah to prophesy and even control nature. (That would explain the many prophetic judgments about natural disasters, like hurricanes, tsunamis, fires and earthquakes, wouldn't it?)

Kabbalah teaches that Hebrew symbols, numbers, letters and words – even the accents on the words – offer hidden meanings. Adherents learn dozens of ways to interpret these meanings, but it's simplists use takes numerical values of words and adds them up to reveal supposed hidden meanings in Scripture. Let me just say this: Jesus didn't say Kabbalah would lead and guide us into all truth. He promised the Holy Spirit would fill that role in His absence (John 16:13). Any other guide is strictly forbidden. Period.

Angel worship is also forbidden. Only the Lord Almighty is worthy of our worship. It's interesting to note that many of the same spirits and heresies written in the Bible remain in the Church today. What we need are more believers to decry them. The Apostles Paul and John left record of the error in angel worship, for example, but are we heeding the warning?

In the Book of Revelation, John fell to his feet to worship an angel who delivered the awe-inspiring message from the Lord. The angel was quick to correct him: "See thou do it not: I am thy fellowservant and of thy brethren that have the testimony of Jesus: worship God: for the testimony of Jesus is the spirit of prophecy" (Revelation 19:10).

The Apostle Paul also had something to say about angel worship:

> Don't tolerate people who try to run your life, ordering you to bow and scrape, insisting that you join their obsession with angels and that you seek out visions. They're a lot of hot air, that's all they are. They're completely out of touch with the source of life, Christ, who puts us together in one piece, whose very breath and blood

flow through us. He is the Head and we are the body.

> Colossians 2:18 (Message)

Oh, but we aren't worshipping angels, you say? Maybe you aren't, but I've read some disturbing accounts recently about an angel who launched a prophetic movement in Kansas City in the 1980s. I've read other accounts of female angels delivering gemstones. Are any of these things biblical? Are there female angels in the Bible. Do angels deliver prosperity gemstones and fill mailboxes with money? Yet some teach these things. Are those who propagate such testimonies out of touch with the source of life, Christ? And, perhaps more importantly, are they leading others into error instead of into righteousness? Are they preaching another gospel?

What of this strange fire within prophetic ministry? The Lord wants our heartfelt worship, our love and our sincere petitions that demonstrate we are leaning and relying on Him. He rejects strange fire. What do I mean by strange fire? One interpretation of strange fire is violating a sacred office through self-exaltation, pride and sin. This was the downfall of Nadab and Abihu, who moved in presumption, moved out of God's timing, failed to sanctify themselves, and fashioned their own strange offering instead of what was commanded (Leviticus 10:1). God judged them because He would not receive an unholy mixture.

So I ask you, what example are we setting for the next generation? Prophets are called to holiness, humility, and should be turning hearts away from sin toward God, not mysticism, angels, or anything else. Yet, we've allowed Kabbalah in churches. We've encouraged angels a place they don't deserve – or even want. We've offered strange fire in the sanctuary. We've watched some in prophetic ministry stray from its purpose, sometimes for the sake of not appearing 'religious.' Yes, we want to make room for God to move how He wants and to avoid the trap of a religious spirit that would quench His operations. But does that mean we throw our discernment out stained glass windows to prove we're open-minded? God forbid.

Chapter 11
The Prophetic Showdown

And Elijah came unto all the people, and said, How long halt ye between two opinions? if the Lord be God, follow him: but if Baal, then follow him. And the people answered him not a word.

1 KINGS 18:21

Could we one day see a face off between holy and unholy prophets? Which side would you be on?

Just like Elijah confronted the prophets of Baal, the time is coming when God's New Testament mouthpieces will confront modern day merchandisers. The true will defy the false. The holy will challenge the unholy. Until that day, spirits of divination, with a little help from the lust of the eyes, the lust of the flesh and the pride of life, are working overtime to woo God's true prophets to the side of err.

Some merchandising prophets, with their miracle water, prophetic soap and prosperity oil, are catching naïve Christians hook, line and sinker. Other Gospel gainsayers are profiting with urgent announcements that God will heal the first five people who run up to the altar with $100 bill in hand.

Money-Hungry Merchandisers

But perhaps the most dangerous merchandisers are those who use their gift to tap into divination. These prophets announce what the believer wants to hear in order to sow a false seed of faith in his heart and reap an improper financial reward, inappropriately earned position or wrongly received recognition. No matter the merchandiser's brand of deceit, it is a practice that stinks in the nostrils of God.

> Then the Lord said, 'These prophets are telling lies in my name. I did not send them or tell them to speak. I did not give them any messages. They prophesy of visions and revelations they have never seen or heard.
>
> They speak foolishness made up in their own lying hearts. Therefore, says the Lord, I will punish these lying prophets, for they have spoken in my name even though I never sent them. They say that no war or famine will come, but they themselves will die by war and famine!
>
> Jeremiah 14:14-15

Of course, most false prophets don't start their ministries as false prophets rather they are tempted and enticed by the idolatry in their hearts. Avoiding Satan's snare begins with the fear of the Lord and the promised wisdom that follows.

After all, the merchandise of wisdom is better than the merchandise of silver, and the gain thereof than fine gold. Wisdom is more precious than rubies and all the things that you can desire are not to be compared to her (Proverbs 3:14-15).

The Way of Escape

The wisdom in God's Word plainly illustrates that with every temptation there is also a way of escape. By comparing the responses of Balaam with Daniel and of Jezebel's diviners with Elijah, we get a clear view of the trap, the way of escape – and the ultimate fate of merchandising prophets.

Remember our discussion of Balaam? Balaam had a clear way of escape: Telling the king's messengers upon their first visit that the Lord forbid him to curse Israel. That would have closed the door to future offers and put an end to the temptation that would lead to his destruction. The end of Balaam came by the command of Moses at the sword of his own people – the Israelites he tried to curse through divination.

Daniel, on the other hand, refused to give in to the temptation presented in King Belshazzar's dilemma. Belshazzar and his guests were drinking from gold and silver cups that his father had stolen from God's temple and giving praises to idols when the fingers of a human hand appeared and wrote on the palace wall. Belshazzar was frightened and summoned enchanters, fortunetellers and diviners to come, promising riches and power to anyone who could interpret it. When none could, the king called Daniel and made him the same offer (Daniel 5).

Daniel was faced with at least three choices at this critical turning point in his ministry. He could accept the king's offer to interpret the message, thereby merchandising his gifting. He could exercise the gift he had freely received from Jehovah to freely interpret the message, all the while knowing that such a harsh word from the Lord could land him in the lion's den. Or he could stand on his credible reputation as God's prophet to falsely interpret the warning message as a blessing message and in all likelihood collect the loot anyway.

Unlike Balaam, Daniel unlocked the hard truth in the writing on the wall. He told the king that his days were numbered and that his kingdom would be divided up and handed over to the enemies. Daniel refused to compromise, no matter the consequences, and God used the king to promote him. As one of his last acts as king, Belshazzar robed him in purple, draped a great gold chain around his neck and positioned him as third-in-charge of the entire kingdom.

A Word About Jezebel's Prophets

King Ahab and his wife Jezebel took the tradition of kings calling on prophets to unlock the mysteries of

God a step further – and a few steps too far. Jezebel had false prophets on her payroll. The wicked queen regularly fed 450 prophets of Baal and 400 prophets of Asherah. Bible scholars estimate that feeding those false prophets cost her about $12,750 a week or $663,000 a year. That's a hefty price tag for a good prophetic word.

So while Jezebel's prophets had full bellies in a time of famine, the queen cut off the prophets of the Lord for fear of the truth (1 Kings 18:4). Obadiah, a type of religious spirit, hid 100 of God's prophets in caves and fed them bread and water. While this may appear like a good work on the surface, Obadiah was only facilitating Jezebel's plan to cut off the uncompromising prophetic word.

While Jezebel's prophets looked well-fed and God's true prophets looked like sheep being led to the slaughter, the story changes in a hurry when Elijah confronts the 850 merchandisers at Mount Carmel in what goes down in Biblical history as the ultimate showdown between the true and the false. Elijah threw down the prophetic gauntlet and challenged the false camp to bring fire down from heaven by calling upon their God. The merchandising diviners cried to Baal from dawn to dusk with no answer.

When the false camp had finally exhausted itself, Elijah built an altar holding a sacrifice to Jehovah, drenched it with four barrels of water, said a simple prayer, and watched as the fire of God fell from heaven and consumed the sacrifice, the wood, the stones, the dust and even the water in the trench. Then Elijah slew his false counterparts one by one. So the ultimate fate of the false prophets came at the hand of the true prophet, who was later taken to heaven in a chariot of fire.

Making a Decision for Christ

Like Old Testament prophets, modern day prophets are also being tempted to merchandise the anointing for fame, fortune or friends in high places. Being plugged into a strong local apostolic church is a safety net because apostles boldly confront false moves of the Spirit and give merchandisers a way of escape by leading them into deep repentance.

The decision to go the way of Baal and or to go the way of Elijah lies in the prophet's heart. If pride, self-will, anger, or lust occupies the place where obedience, love and truth should live, then the merchandising prophet may succeed in reaping worldly rewards for a season but the retirement fund built on ill-gotten gains leads only to death (Romans 6:23).

While there is certainly abundant grace for the true prophet who misses it, the Book of Revelation makes it clear that the false prophets (those who purposely set out to lie and deceive God's people) will be cast into the lake of fire and brimstone and be tormented day and night forever and ever (Revelation 20:10).

I hope this book stirred your heart to fulfill the prophetic call of God on your life and to keep your heart clean. My heart's desire is to see the glorious Church without spot or wrinkle come into manifestation.

That's going to require saints who are equipped for the work of the ministry. That is going to require apostles, evangelists, pastors, teachers – and prophets – who are determined to stand up for truth. It may get darker in the days ahead. It may get more difficult to stand in the office of the prophet. If our heartbeat is one with God's, then we will be thrilled to hear him say, "Well done thou good and faithful servant" (Matthew 25:23).

Afterword

Create in Me a Clean Heart

The Old Testament is full of the stories of great heroes and great failures – and sometimes the same person filled both shoes. We are no different today. We all make mistakes. Some are just bigger and more visible than others. Thank God for His grace and mercy that restores us when we turn to the right or the left of His will. I suppose you could sum up the entire book this way: the heart of the prophetic possesses a fear of the Lord.

I believe we need to pray for a fear of the Lord to come upon us. I believe we need to pray for a spirit of wisdom and revelation in the knowledge of Jesus, the eyes of our understanding being enlightened that we may know the hope of His calling (Ephesians 1:17-19). I believe we need to pray that we may live a life worthy of the Lord and may please Him in every way: bearing fruit in every good work, growing in the knowledge of God (Colossians 1:10).

If we really understood the magnitude of wearing the prophetic mantle, we would spend much more time on our face than on our platforms. There is a need for brokenness in the prophetic ministry today as the Lord looks for those with clean hearts that can receive, bear and transmit His truth. It takes a clean heart to deliver a pure word. If the word of the Lord settles into a heart full of malice, greed or control, then it may well be profaned.

We need to cry out for clean hearts, for the heart of the prophetic is a clean one. Forgive yourself. Forgive those who have wronged you. Forgive God if you feel you need to (though God does nothing that needs to be forgiven). Walk in love, so that all men might know that you are Christ's disciples. We can pray David's petition right now, the cry for mercy after the Prophet Nathan exposed his sin. We find this beautiful prayer in Psalm 51 of the New International Version of the Bible:

> Have mercy on me, O God, according to your unfailing love; according to your great compassion blot out my transgressions. Wash away all my iniquity and cleanse me from my sin. For I know my transgressions, and my sin is always before me. Against you, you only, have I sinned and done what is evil in your sight, so that you are proved right when you speak and justified when you judge.
>
> Surely I was sinful at birth, sinful from the time my mother conceived me. Surely you desire truth in the inner parts; you teach me wisdom in the inmost place. Cleanse me with hyssop, and I will be clean; wash me, and I will be whiter

than snow. Let me hear joy and gladness; let the bones you have crushed rejoice. Hide your face from my sins and blot out all my iniquity.

Create in me a pure heart, O God, and renew a steadfast spirit within me. Do not cast me from your presence or take your Holy Spirit from me. Restore to me the joy of your salvation and grant me a willing spirit, to sustain me. Then I will teach transgressors your ways, and sinners will turn back to you. Save me from bloodguilt, O God, the God who saves me, and my tongue will sing of your righteousness.

O Lord, open my lips, and my mouth will declare your praise. You do not delight in sacrifice, or I would bring it; you do not take pleasure in burnt offerings. The sacrifices of God are a broken spirit; a broken and contrite heart, O God, you will not despise. In your good pleasure make Zion prosper; build up the walls of Jerusalem. Then there will be righteous sacrifices, whole burnt offerings to delight you; then bulls will be offered on your altar.

Amen and amen.

I'll admit, it can be discouraging at times to see some put a blight on prophetic ministry with their merchandising, judgments and curses. Truthfully, I cringe every time I read about well-known merchandisers rolling through town under the guise of a revival to drain the coffers of the region's local church members. And I feel downright nauseous when I watch prophets claim credit for predicting a natural disaster and calling it the wrath of God. I know you are, too.

Despite it all, though, I remain encouraged. There is a bright future for the prophetic ministry. The Lord has opened my eyes, and I pray that He will open yours. What do I see? Well, I see that spirits of divination, religion, witchcraft, Jezebel, religion, Baal and their wicked cohorts are waging war against the prophetic ministry in this hour, to discredit it and delay the glorious Church. But, more importantly, I also see this: they that be with us are more than they that be with them (2 Kings 6:16). I see horses and chariots of fire round about the Melchizedek prophets. I see prophets turning hearts, preparing the way, reforming, standing in the gap, making up the hedge – fulfilling their destinies and leaving legacies. I see you being all God called you to be.

God has a purpose for prophetic ministry and He needs His prophets willing to walk worthy of the vocation (Ephesians 4:1). Will you accept the challenge to come to new levels of accuracy in the prophetic? With it comes a dare to examine yourself, empty yourself, and fill yourself with the Spirit of God. Like John the Baptist, we must decrease that Jesus might increase (John 3:30). I pray what I have written on the pages that make up this book will serve as a prophetic wake up call to all of us and, in some small way, contribute to the complete restoration of vital prophetic ministry in purity and humility. He that has ears let him hear (Matthew 11:15).

Hallelujah! Let the prophets arise and go forth with clean hearts in the spirit of Elijah!

ABOUT THE AUTHOR

Jennifer LeClaire is a prophetic voice and teacher whose passion is to see the lost come to Christ and equip believers to understand the will and ways of God. She carries a reforming voice that seeks to turn hearts to the Lord and edify the Body of Christ.

Jennifer has a powerful testimony of God's power to set the captives free and claim beauty for ashes. She shares her story with women who need to understand the love and grace of God in a lost and dying world.

Jennifer is news editor at Charisma magazine, as well as a prolific author who has written several books, including "The Heart of the Prophetic," "A Prophet's Heart," "Doubtless: Faith that Overcomes the World," and "Fervent Faith: Discover how a fervent spirit is a defense against the devil." Her materials have been translated into several languages. Some of her work is archived in the Flower Pentecostal Heritage Museum.

Other Books by Jennifer LeClaire

The Heart of the Prophetic: Keys to flowing in a more powerful prophetic anointing

Faith Magnified

Fervent Faith: Discover how a fervent spirit is a defense against the devil.

Did the Spirit of God Say That?

Breakthrough!

The Making of a Prophet

The Spiritual Warrior's Guide to Defeating Jezebel

Visit Jennifer online at:

www.jenniferleclaire.org

www.facebook.com/propheticbooks

www.twitter.com/propheticbooks

www.youtube.com/jnleclaire

www.flickr.com/propheticbooks

www.myspace.com/propheticbooks

www.connect.tangle.com/propheticbooks

www.ingramcontent.com/pod-product-compliance
Lightning Source LLC
LaVergne TN
LVHW051509070426
835507LV00022B/3016